SR-71 Blackbird

in action

by Lou Drendel
illustrated by Lou Drendel

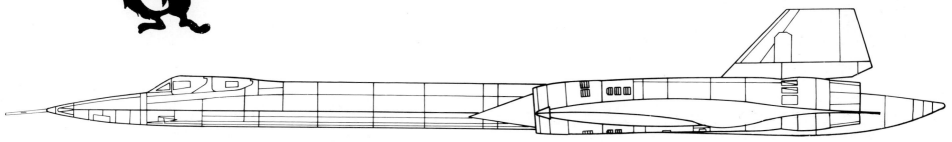

Aircraft No. 55

squadron/signal publications

An SR-71A of the 9th SRW at 85,000 feet, flashing across the sky at the speed of a bullet, covering 35 miles per minute, and surveying a 60 mile wide swath with it's sophisticated reconnaissance sensors.

ISBN 0-89747-136-9

If you have any photographs of the aircraft, armor, soldiers or ships of any nation, particularly wartime snapshots, why not share them with us and help make Squadron/Signal's books all the more interesting and complete in the future. Any photograph sent to us will be copied and the original returned. The donor will be fully credited for any photos used. Please send them to: Squadron/Signal Publication, Inc., 1115 Crowley Dr., Carrollton, Texas 75011-5010.

PHOTO CREDITS

USAF
NASA
Lockheed
John Andrews
Charles B. Mayer
Michel C. Klaver
John Mallozzi

Norman E. Taylor
David Menard
James Goodall
Jerry Geer
Ted Carlson
Paul Stevens

Forward

It is cold up here. At least minus 60 degrees Centigrade most of the time. There is not a lot of weather. Clouds almost never get within 10,000 feet of this altitude. You can see almost forever...even make out the curvature of the earth. The sky is very, very dark blue. Ultramarine. You can see the stars at any time of the day. Not much air up here either. Humans can't survive up here without pressurization. Their blood would boil instantly, and their skin would flake off like a just-right pie crust. Not that we see many humans up here. Oh, we get the occasional astronaut or cosmonaut coming or going. And the teeming masses down there do keep sending up weather balloons, trying to figure out what the jet stream has in store for them.

There are some people who do come through fairly regularly. They are members of the 9th Strategic Reconnaissance Wing, which is part of the United States Air Force. They are home-based at Beale Air Force Base in California, but I have heard that they operate world-wide from what they euphemistically term their 'Forward Operating Locations'. About half of them mosey along nice and slow, taking time to get a good look at the scenery. These sedate gents fly what they call the U-2, or more familiarly, 'The Dragon Lady'.

The other half of this group hardly gives you a chance to see them coming before they are gone. They fly the SR-71, and it moves through here at better than the muzzle velocity of a 30.06 bullet. Whole lot faster than those transient astros too! I hear there are only a few of them...probably not more than a couple of dozen pairs. Did I mention that? They come in pairs, a Pilot and a Reconnaissance Systems Operator. Man, do they come through! If that SR-71 wasn't so big, you might never see them. You'd know they had been through though. There is that thunderclap of a triple-sonic boom, followed by a blast of heat radiating from black skin that reaches temperatures of 1100 degrees Fahrenheit. At night, the tailpipes glowing white hot can be seen for a long ways off. The rest of the airplane ranges from about 450 to 550 degrees. Friction does that. You can't move through the air...even as little air as there is up here...at better than Mach three for extended periods without causing lots of friction.

Yessir, that SR-71 is some airplane! Oh, I know there are others that have flown faster. We used to see the X-15 come through here on it's way to lots higher and goin' lots faster. And there are those astronauts with their spacecrafts...why, they even got one now that sort of looks like an airplane! Course, whenever we have seen it, it is either acting like a regular spacecraft, riding a rocket, or impersonating a rock.

But that SR-71 is pure airplane. Fastest airplane in the world. It doesn't just go fast in spurts either. It takes off under it's own power, gets up here, settles into Mach three plus, and keeps on keepin' on at that rate! We haven't seen another airplane that could do that. The secret of that extended Mach three performance is in the engines. Those J-58's get downright economical to operate once you get them going fast enough to turn into ramjets! Up here, the engine only produces about 17% of the thrust, with the inlet producing 58% and the exhaust producing the rest. Put that economy together with 80,000 pounds of fuel in a 60,000 pound airframe and you get some pretty amazing ranges.

Sure sounds like something out of Buck Rogers in the 21st Century, doesn't it? Well, the amazin' thing is, the SR and it's cousins been doin' this for *at least twenty years!* Makes you wonder if maybe there was some kind of a time warp back there in the late fifties-early sixties, when those 150 or so hand-picked engineers in Kelly Johnson's Skunk Works at Lockheed turned out this airplane. Maybe there was. Lockheed's manufacturing numbers for the SR-71 series start with 2001.

Introduction

The problem with doing a book on a subject that has remained classified for all of it's career, and continues to be one of the most sensitive military areas, is that there is very little 'official' information available. Throughout this book, you will read such phrases as 'reportedly', 'speculation is', 'common knowledge', or 'maybe', 'probably', and 'perhaps'. Information that is officially disseminated on most other major aircraft programs is still a closely held secret in the case of the SR-71 and it's forerunners.

After months of sifting through magazine articles, newspaper stories, and transcripts of personal interviews and a trip to Beale AFB, I have tried to put together the most accurate picture of the development and operational use of the Blackbirds possible. However, lacking official confirmation of much of the basic research information, it is impossible to present this book as gospel. Where confirmation is lacking, I have tried to indicate that with the above mentioned euphemisms. At some future date much of the following may be verified or vilified. In the meantime, it is as accurate a picture as I could possibly paint of the mysterious and marvelous Blackbird.

The first public acknowledgment of the existence of the Blackbird came on February 29, 1964. Barry Goldwater, the frontrunner for the Republican nomination to run for President, was accusing President Johnson of being more interested in social legislation for the Great Society than in the defense of America. LBJ, in an effort to deflect Goldwater's criticism, decided to take some of the wraps off of what had been one of the most closely held secrets in America. The fact that the program had been ininitiated in the Eisenhower Administration, and brought to fruition in the Kennedy Administration didn't prevent LBJ from claiming credit for it.

The aircraft announced by LBJ was the **YF-12A**. He stated that: "The performance of the A-11 far exceeds that of any other aircraft in the world today." Cruising speeds in excess of Mach 3, at altitudes over 70,000 feet were attributed to the new design. At the time of the announcement, no Air Force fighter designation existed for Lockheed's revolutionary design. Reportedly, LBJ misread 'AMI' (Advanced Manned Interceptor) as 'A-11', and this was allowed to stand (it was known that Lockheed's designations for the design evolution of the Blackbird ran from **A-1** to **A-12**, which lent additional credence to the A-11 designation.) If this is true, then LBJ can claim some sort of record for misstatement, for when he followed up his February 29 A-11 announcement with a July 25 revelation of the development of the SR-71, he juxtaposed Reconnaissance Strike (RS-70, as the ill-fated XB-70 was to have been operationally known.) into Strike Reconnaissance. The announcement of the SR-71 was blatant political hay-making. The Republican Convention was in session in San Francisco, and its speakers had criticized LBJ for concentrating on missiles rather than developing a new manned bomber. The Republican Platform charged that the Johnson administration had failed to initiate a single new major strategic weapon system. Since the cancelled RS-70 had been meant to operate as a *Strategic Reconnaissance* strike aircraft, it was not unreasonable to assume that it's only other companion in Mach 3 land might not do the same. And to solidify this impression, SR: Strike-Reconnaissance, became SR: Strategic Reconnaissance.

The first public showing of a Blackbird was in the fall of 1964, at Edwards AFB, California. The YF-12A was the interceptor which would guard our shores from the hordes of Russian bombers poised just over the horizon. It was widely reported as being the follow-on to the ill-fated North American F-108 Rapier, which was to have been the escort for our own hordes of RS-70's. The YF-12A did, in fact, use the Hughes ASG-18 radar and the GAR-9 missiles that had been developed for the F-108. Three YF-12A's were in conspicuous evidence at various times during a test program that seemed strangely sporadic to some aerospace reporters of that time. The press reported that other 'A-11s' were being tested at a secret site in Nevada. (Possibly Watertown Strip at Groom Dry Lake, also known as 'The Ranch') The YF-12 testing took place at Edwards AFB, California. In addition to the three YF-12A (serial numbers 06934, 35, 36) and the SR-71 prototype, which was modified from YF-12A 06937, a further eight were reported to have been constructed. In

The sharply pointed nose of the CIA's A-12 is one of the principle differences between it and the SR-71. The surviving A-12s are stored at Lockheed's Palmdale facility. They carry no markings, but exhibit the natural metal that most carried during their operational careers, with Black paint applied only to the areas that attained the highest in-flight temperatures. (John Andrews)

fact, there were no other YF-12s, and the reason that their test program was not pursued feverishly was probably that the operational mission of the Blackbirds was never meant to be anything but clandestine reconnaissance. By the time that the airplane was revealed to the public, the test program was well advanced. Lockheed's test pilots, headed by Louis W. Schalk, and including William C. Park, Robert J. Gilliland, and James D. Eastham had conducted such an outstanding test program that they received, as a group, the Society of Experimental Test Pilots' Iven C. Kincheloe award for 1964.

A-12 Development

The first Blackbirds were cloaked in secrecy at that time, and to this day remain an enigma. The Blackbird was designed as a follow-on to the U-2, at the behest of the CIA and with CIA funds. Shortly after the U-2 began flying operational missions, it became obvious that the high-flying, but slow, U-2 would become increasingly vulnerable to some sort of anti-aircraft system, whether air-to-air or surface-to-air. Lockheed was already working on possible solutions when Kelly Johnson, head of Lockheed's advanced development Projects (Skunk Works), was summoned to Washington in 1958. A competition to develop the successor to the U-2 was initiated, with Lockheed's designs being evaluated as superior to those of Convair or the Navy. The contract was given to Lockheed in 1959, and the first flight of the A-12 took place on April 26, 1962. Eighteen A-12's were built for the CIA. They are serial numbers 06924 through 33, and 06938 through 41 (06934 through 37 were developed into USAF YF-l2s and SR-71s). The principle difference between the A-12 and follow-on Blackbirds is that the A-12 was a single seat aircraft, with recon equipment occupying what became the Fire Control Officer (FCO) in the YF-12 or Reconnaissance Systems Officer (RSO) seat in the SR-71.

Preliminary design work on the CIA's A-12 was well underway when Francis Gary Powers and his U-2 were shot down over central Russia on May Day, 1960. The resulting international uproar caused cancellation of an impending summit meeting between President Eisenhower and Russian Premier Kruschev. Reportedly, it also ultimately elicited a promise from Ike, to Kruschev, never to overfly Soviet territory again. There is no evidence to suggest that the CIA ever broke that promise with their A-12's. In fact, there is no public evidence to suggest that the CIA even flew the A-12 operationally! Most speculation would have you believe that they did, in fact, operate on a world-wide basis with their Blackbirds. But there is also evidence that at least half of the A-12 fleet was stored inside a hangar at Palmdale subsequent to development testing. Whether or not the CIA did operate it's A-12s operationally may remain a mystery for years to come. There are currently eight aircraft in storage at Palmdale, with six unaccounted for. Were these six *all* lost in the test program? Or operationally? What happened to the pilots? These and other questions regarding the blackest of the Blackbirds may not be answered for years to come, but when they are, what great war stories they will make!

In September, 1964 Kelly Johnson received the Collier Trophy for his design work on the Blackbird. The ceremony was held at the White House, and was followed shortly thereafter by a public demonstration of the YF-12A at Edwards AFB. It was the first close-up look at the YF-12A for the press, and resulted in a blizzard of publicity which reinforced the interceptor mission for the Blackbird. The speculation about just exactly how fast and how high the Blackbird would fly was heightened by all of this publicity. It was satisfied on May 1, 1965, when the YF-12A was flown to nine new records for speed and altitude. The USAF team of pilots was lead by Colonel Robert L. 'Silver Fox' Stephens, the first military pilot to fly the YF-12.

Stephens, with his Fire Control Officer (FCO), Lt. Col. Daniel Andre, averaged 2,062 MPH (Mach 3.17) in out-and-back runs over the 15/25 kilometer straight-away course to set an absolute world speed record, as well as a new jet class record. They also set the records for absolute sustained altitude (80,000 feet), and jet class altitude record.

The other Air Force pilot was Major Walter F. Daniel, who teamed with two Fire Control Officers, Major Noel T. Warner, and Captain James Cooney to set records for the 1,000 and 500 kilometer closed course. The YF-12A also set records with 1,000 and 2,000 kilogram payloads that day. These records had previously been held by the Soviet Union's E-266, a pre-production development version of the Mig-25.

06937, the prototype SR-71 made it's first flight on December 22,1964. Production versions of the SR-71 were delivered to the Air Force beginning in January, 1966. Lockheed's production number for the SR-71 begins with the number 2001, which is serial number 17950, and runs consecutively through 2032, serial number 17981.

The 9th Strategic Reconnaissance Wing was organized effective June 25, 1966 as the unit to fly the SR-71. The 9th's history dates to the days when the only military aircraft were flown by the Signal Corps.

The 9th traces it's component squadrons, the 1st and the 99th, to pre-World War I. The 1st was organized in 1913 to assist General Pershings's 2nd Army Division guard the Mexican border. It is a significant fact of it's history that the first ever American military reconnaissance flight was flown by a Curtiss Flyer over France in 1916 by the 9th. The 1st and 99th Squadrons flew combat missions over France throughout World War I. After World War I they were reorganized as the 9th Bombardment Group.

The group flew B-29's during World War II, and was inactivated at the end of the war, only to be reactivated within a year as the 9th Strategic Reconnaissance Group. In April, 1950 the wing was redesignated the 9th Bombardment Group and given B-47's, and a change of base, from Fairfield-Suisun AFB, California (Travis AFB), to Mountain Home AFB. While at Mountain Home, the 9th made the longest non-stop point-to-point flight that any SAC aircraft had attempted to that date. Using aerial refuelling, the B-47's of the

One of the few A-12s which were painted nearly all-black. The sharper nose profile, with more triangular-shaped chines are most evident in this view. Also of interest in an apparent flight test camera housing at the rear of the fuselage. The direction in which it is pointing indicates that it may have been mounted to record the launching of the D-21 Drone. (See page 22) (USAF)

9th flew 8,300 miles, from Mountain Home to New Zealand.

Titan missles began to arrive at Mountain Home in 1961, and the 9th was redesignated the 9th Strategic Aerospace Wing. When the Tactical Air Command was slated for Mountain Home in 1966, it meant another inactivation for the 9th.

When it was decided that the SR-71 would go into SAC's operational inventory, Beale AFB, California was chosen as it's home base. The 4200th Strategic Reconnaissance Wing was activated on January 1, 1965. The 4200th would be the training wing for the SR-71, and to accomodate the special requirements of SR training, the Air Force spent $9 million to build new hangars, fuel storage facilities, a physiological building, new parking ramp, engine test stand, and runway arresting barrier. The first SR-71A was delivered in January, and was followed a few days later by the first of two SR-71B's. The 4200th was inactivated on June 22, 1966, and the 9th Strategic Reconnaissasnce Wing, with the 1st and 99th Strategic Reconnaissance Squadrons was activated. The 9th Wing would accomplish all of the training, and conduct operational missions from it's headquarters at Beale.

On April 17, 1967 the Silver Fox climbed into an SR-71 and made the longest Mach 3 flight in history. Their flight of over 14,000 miles earned the FAI's Gold Medal for Colonel Robert L. Stephens and his RSO, Lt. Col. Kenneth D. Hurley. The tremendous speed and range of the SR-7l gave SAC a reconnaissance capability that was so far removed from any previous systems that it's implications were staggering. The SR-71 could survey a strip of ground 30 miles wide, from Sacramento to Washington, D.C., *in an hour!*

While the SR-71 was becoming operational, the YF-12's were winding up a test program that was so successful that the 500 man unit was awarded the Air Force Outstanding Unit Citation. This program had been conducted by personnel from Air Force Systems Command, SAC, and Air Defense Command. The YF-12's went into flyable storage at the end of this program, and remained inactive until NASA expressed an interest in using them to do SST research. (There was absolutely no doubt in anyone's mind at that point in time...the late 60's...that the United States would have the worlds best Supersonic Transport. And most people also believed we would win the Vietnam War.)

YF-12A number 06935 blasted off the runway at Edwards on December 11, 1969, on the first phase of it's born-again test program. The initial phase of this program was under the aegis of the Air Force, and included test objectives aimed at answering some questions about implementation of the B-1, which was as sure a thing as the SST, they thought. On this first flight, the YF-12 climbed to 75,000 feet, accelerated out to Mach 3, then successfully intercepted a B-57 which was flying at 30,000 feet and Mach 0.5, effectively verifying the status of the radar. Air Force objectives for it's portion of the tests included exploration of it's use in a tactical environment, how AWACS would control supersonic aircraft, and how YF-12 programs could be adapted to the B-1 development program.

The NASA tests would answer questions such as how engine inlet performance affected airframe and propulsion interaction, boundary layer noise, heat transfer under high mach conditions, and altitude hold at supersonic speeds would also be investigated. The NASA budget for the 2½ year program was $14 million, of which $4 million came from excess funds from the X-15 and XB-70 programs. The Air Force portion of the program was budgeted at $4 million.

The U.S. Advanced Supersonic Technology Program, conducted by NASA's Flight Research Center at Edwards AFB also used the SR-71 prototype, 06937, in tests that lasted far longer than the originally intended 2½ year program. The two Blackbirds averaged 6 months per year of ground time, during which instrumentation packages were developed or removed and analyzed. While on flight status, the two aircraft averaged one flight per week, usually generating enough new data to require several days of analyzation and instrument recalibration. One of the first discoveries made was that, unlike the triplesonic airflow generated in wind tunnels, the Mach 3 airflow over the airframe surfaces in flight was smooth. Data gathered in early test flights enabled aerodynamicists to design high mach number wind tunnels that were free of the normal disturbances.

The altitude-hold problem concerned not only the YF-12/SR-71 aircraft. It had also been encountered by the Anglo-French Concorde SST, and would be a major problem for the U.S. SST. Altitude excursions of up to ± 3,000 feet were encountered at high altitude and high mach numbers. Temperature variations, which were totally unpredictable, were thought to be the cause of these oscillations, and a computer that would connect autopilot to engine and inlet controls was the proposed solution.

While the USAF and NASA test programs proceeded, and were high-profile Blackbird operations, the 9th SRW was flying operational SR-71 recon missions world-wide. All of the world's hot spots came under Blackbird surveillance. Vietnam, the Middle East, Cuba all were photographed on a regular basis by SR-71s flying from bases in England, Okinawa, and Thailand. Most of the time, the Air Force managed to keep a tight lid on the activities of the SR-71 force. Occasionally, the lid was lifted just high enough to afford a glimpse into the nether world of Electronic Intelligence (ELINT) missions.

As President Nixon was preparing to shock the world with his opening to China in 1971, the 9th SRW was completing a detailed mapping of the Chinese mainland. This had involved literally hundreds of overflights (500 official protests had been made by the Peking Government), and years of effort. As a quid pro quo for his trip to China, President Nixon reportedly promised to stop the SR-71 overflights. Aviation Week reported in November, 1971 that *unmanned* reconnaissance flights were continuing over the Chinese mainland.

A 1972 Ramparts Magazine article quoted a former Air Force sergeant, who had worked for the National Security Agency, as saying that there was virtually no way that the SR-71 could be brought down. He mentioned specific instances of attempted Chinese interceptions in which the Mig-21s that had scrambled to intercept the Blackbird were left looking at each other, and wondering what had happened to their quarry. He also asserted that SR-71's had overflown Russian airspace, while NSA listening posts on the borders of the USSR monitored Soviet air defense reaction. According to the 26-year old former USAF sergeant, the ELINT capabilities of the United States allowed them to keep track of virtually all Soviet military aircraft, and even to determine who was flying them at any given time. The SR-71 was an important part of this overall capability.

In an October 15, 1973 article, U. S. News and World Report stated that; "Fewer than 10 of the 24.6 million dollar airplanes are still on duty. The rest of the original two wings — several dozen planes — have been put into mothballs." The main thrust of this article was

There was a two seat version of the A-12, used for pilot training. This one is in storage at Palmdale. (John Andrews)

to write the epitaph of the manned reconnaissance airplane, and specifically, the SR-71. Where they got their figure of 24.6 million dollars is not known. Other sources have indicated that the initial cost of the airframe alone was probably close to $50 million 1963 dollars, and that did not include avionics or engines. There were, of course, never two wings of SR-71s, and there were less than three dozen built. Their figure of less than 10 operational aircraft may have been close to accurate, but their assertion that the SR-71 was about to be retired was as inaccurate as the rest of their article. Indications are that the SR-71 will still be flying operational missions well into the 1980's. Remotely Piloted Vehicles, (RPVs) which were supposed to have replaced the SR-71 and U-2 recon programs, have been shrouded in even more secrecy than the Blackbirds.

Protests of overflights were not limited to the Chinese. In October of 1973, at the height of the Yom Kippur War, the Egyptian government registered a detailed protest of a violation of Egyptian airspace which could only have been accomplished by aircraft of a type possessed by the United States exclusively. The Egyptian communique said, "The two reconnaissance planes violated Egyptian airspace at 1105 GMT, 13 October, 1973, over Port Said, went deep into Egypt at Nagaa Hammady, 590 kilometers south of Cairo, turned back over the capital and flew eastward in the direction of Jordan and Syria, then back to the Mediterranean Sea. This is the first time Egypt's airspace has been violated by this type of plane." Whether or not it was the first time that SR-71s had overflown Egypt is open to debate. It was obviously the first time that they had been detected by the Egyptians.

Public consciousness of the Blackbirds was raised considerably by several record-breaking and setting flights during the 1970s.

In April, 1971 USAF Lt. Cols Thomas B. Estes and Dewain C. Vick flew back and forth across the United States twice, and made a complete circle of the Western states in under 10½ hours. The flight covered a distance of 15,000 miles and earned them the Harmon and Mackay Trophies for their efforts.

One of the most highly publicised flights ever made by the Blackbird came in September, 1974. The then-existing record time for a flight from New York to London was 4 hours and 40 minutes, set by a Royal Navy F-4K Phantom in 1969. The USAF decided to break the record. Considering the new record time, "break" hardly seems an adequate description of what they did to the old record.

Nacelle and wing detail of the A-12. Taped over areas under nacelle are blow-in doors. This aircraft appears to have black wing leading edges, while most of the fuselage and center-wing sections are painted black underneath. (John Andrews)

The A-12s stored at Palmdale have had their rudders removed. (John Andrews)

Manning their Blackbird at 2330 local time, amid the din from the un-muffled twin Buick V-8 engines used to provide starting power for the Blackbird's J-58s, Major James V. Sullivan, pilot, and Major Noel F. Widdifield, RSO, began a five hour and forty five minute flight that would amaze the world.

Lifting off from Beale two minutes into September 1, SR-71A Serial number 17972 climbed into the refuelling track 26,000 feet above Nevada. After taking on a full load from the KC-135Q, The Blackbird climbed and accelerated to Mach 3 as it crossed the United States. One more refuelling was required, and it took place off the coast of the Carolinas. With this rendezvous complete, Sullivan advanced the throttles and once more headed upward into Mach 3 country, passing through the timing gate east of New York on speed, and on course.

Exactly 1 hour, fifty five minutes, and forty two seconds later the SR-71 passed through the timing gate in mid-Channel, off Southhampton, completing the run in less than a seventeenth of the time it had taken Charles Lindbergh some forty seven years earlier. Sadly, Lindbergh had died less than a week before and so did not see yet another tribute to his pioneering spirit.

After remaining on static display for a week at the Farnborough International Air Show, the SR-71 was flown to Mildenhall to be prepared for the return flight to Beale. A record was established on this flight. (No previous record existed.) Captain Harold B. Adams, pilot, and Major William C. Machurek, RSO took off from Mildenhall, climbed to refuelling rendezvous, and after taking on fuel, climbed and accelerated as they crossed the Atlantic. A second refuelling was required over Goose Bay, Labrador before the final Mach 3 dash across Canada and into the United States. *Decel/descent* was planned for a point 200 miles northeast of Los Angeles, which would have gotten the Blackbird subsonic 40 miles short of all that glass and those sensitive eardrums. An engine compressor stall during this phase of the flight caused the Blackbird to boom the suburbs of LA, which resulted in some damage claims. When the Blackbird passed through the LA timing gate, it had covered a distance of 5,645 miles in 3 hours, 47 minutes for an average speed of 1,435 MPH. Nearly an hour and fifteen minutes of that time had been spent at subsonic speed.

More records were set in 1976. On July 27 and 28 operational crews and aircraft from Beale virtually wiped everyone else's name from the record books. The three crews who set the records were Majors Adolphus H. Bledsoe, Jr., pilot and John T. Fuller, RSO, Captain Robert C. Helt, pilot, and Major Larry A. Elliott, RSO, and Captain Eldon W. Joersz, pilot, and Major George T. Morgan, RSO. All flights were from Beale, and the records were certified by the FAI with equipment at Edwards AFB, where the record portion of the flights took place.

The 9th SRW had been functioning as a single squadron wing (the 1st SRS) for several years, when further budgetary considerations forced a merger with the 100th SRW in 1976. The 100th had been operating U-2s and Ryan AQM-34 RPVs, supported by DC-130s and CH-3s at Davis Monthan AFB. Transfer of the RPVs to TAC left the 100th as another single squadron wing, and prompted SAC to merge them into a single wing. The U-2s moved to Beale, and the 99th SRS was reactivated. The 100th wing also moved to Beale, but became the 100th Aerial Refueling Wing, with two squadrons of KC-135Qs, which support the SR-71 world-wide. While the personnel of the 100th transferred into the 99th SRS, the personnel for the 100th were drawn from the 17th Bombardment Wing, which had lost it's B-52's to other units earlier in the year. The 9th SRW was put in the unique position of operating the fastest and slowest of Strategic Reconnaissance aircraft. Though there is the natural rivalry and verbal jousting between SR-71 and U-2 squadrons, there has been no other fall-out from this unusual situation.

The SR-71 has continued to make headlines. In 1979 President Carter sent it into action over Cuba to monitor the "unacceptable" Russian combat brigade. Time Magazine reported in October, 1979 that the Blackbirds had also flown over Cuba in 1978 to investigate the presence of MiG-23s. Time also credited the SR-71 with the ability to "efface it's image from watching radar screens." Also according to Time, Russian missiles had attempted to shoot down the Blackbirds in several other parts of the world, including Eastern Europe, the Middle East, and North Korea....all without success.

In the fall of 1981 a Kadena-based SR-71 was fired at by a North Korean SAM battery as it flew off the coast of North Korea. Newsweek called it "a spitball probe of U.S. resolve." Though the SAM didn't come close to hitting the SR-71, U.S. reaction was quick and tough sounding. U.S. representatives called for a meeting of the Military Armistice Commission, which oversees relations between North and South Korea, and State Department Spokesman Dean Fischer asserted that the North Korean action violated accepted norms of international behavior. He further stated that the United States would take whatever steps were necessary to ensure the safety of our pilots and planes. Presumably, that would include destruction of any threatening SAM sites.

The complete history of Blackbird operation will not be written for years to come. When it is, it will read like a geographical who's who — a tour of every corner of the earth, encountering situations and making discoveries that will have changed the course of history. The pilots who flew the airplane will have stories to tell that will be hair-raising, at least, and those who made the ultimate sacrifice can be honored publicly. Until that day comes, we can only speculate on what the SR-71 has done, where it has gone, and how it's missions have affected history. Chances are, none of the speculation will come close to the truth.

Developments

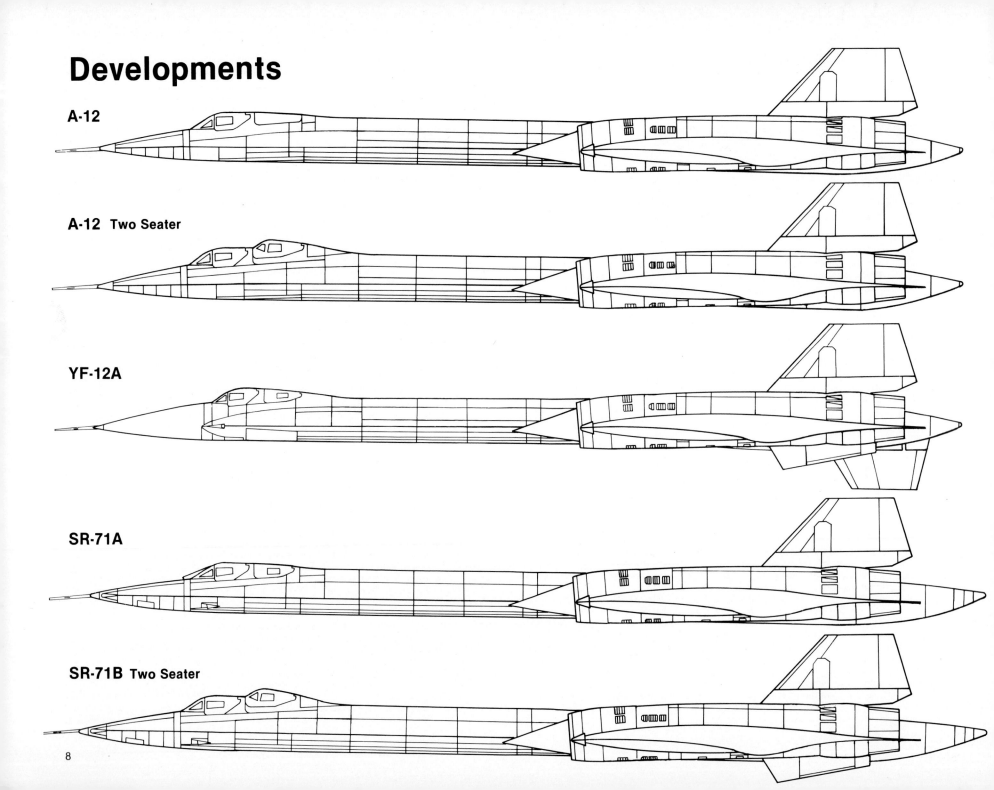

A-12

A-12 Two Seater

YF-12A

SR-71A

SR-71B Two Seater

The Design

I believe I can truly say that everything on the aircraft, from rivets and fluids, up through materials and power plants had to be invented from scratch.
Clarence L. 'Kelly' Johnson (from a presentation to an AIAA Aircraft and Design Operations Meeting.)

To say that the Blackbird is the product of design genius is an understatement...and not quite accurate. The Blackbird is the product of the collective design genius of Lockheed's famous "Skunk Works", the Advanced Development Projects Group, which gave birth to the U-2 and the F-104, among other notable designs. Though the Skunk Works has enjoyed a reputation for innovation and accomplishment, they have not received half the credit due them for their work on the Blackbird. That has been due to the secrecy surrounding it's development and operational use.

In this age of high speed computers, capable of sophisticated design verification projections, it is sometimes forgotten that the Skunk Works had to develop the Blackbird with the tool of the pre-computer age.....the slide rule. It was a time-consuming, expensive, and sometimes exasperating method of pioneering. The fact that the Blackbird is still the only airplane in the world capable of sustained speeds in excess of Mach 3 plus, at altitudes of 85,000 feet or more is a tribute to the perseverance and creative genius of Kelly Johnson and his hand-picked Skunk Works team.

The design configuration of the Blackbird is a modified, tailless delta, with blended forward wing, called a chine. The chine acts as a fixed canard and the lift it produces at cruise speeds reduces the forward fuselage bending moment to half and decreases drag. The effective integration of the blended-body into the Blackbird is most evident by the design modifications that must be made when the integrity of the design is interrupted. For instance, incorporation of the radome housing the ASG-18 fire control radar in the YF-12, which resulted in cut-back of the chine, necessitated addition of three ventral fins to ensure that directional stability was maintained at high speed. The second, raised, cockpit of the SR-71B trainer required addition of two ventral fins for the same reason.

The high temperatures of Mach three plus flight, endured for long periods of time, were the source of a large percentage of the design difficulties. The first assumption made in designing a high speed anything is that you need as smooth a surface as possible to reduce drag. But when heat was applied to smooth wing panels, they behaved like potato chips. Eventually the chordwise corrugations that are such a recognizable feature of the Blackbirds were added. Not only do they add strength and stability to the wing, they also provide additional surface to radiate heat, with very little penalty in drag.

The conical camber incorporated in the leading edge of the outboard wing sections reduce bending moment and torsion. The vertical stablizers are all moving. Conventional rudders were considered, but found wanting because they lacked the authority for directional control in a single engine situation. The all-moving surfaces are two and a half times more effective than conventional rudders, and require less deflection, which means less drag. They are canted inward at 15 degrees, and have a maximum movement of ± 20 degrees. A benefit of the inward-canted verticals is reduction of the rolling moment due to sideslip and vertical deflection. This is evident at both ends of the speed spectrum. Their effectiveness is further attested to by the Blackbird's ability to handle cross winds of up to 35 knots at 90 degrees to runway heading.

Wind tunnel testing revealed that there was no appreciable advantage to incorporating flaps or leading edge devices to the basic design. The large wing area generates a healthy ground-effect cushion as it approaches the runway, making slick landings easy. Four elevon surfaces, two outboard of the nacelles, and two inboard, act as elevators and ailerons. Aileron deflection is ± 12 degrees.

At Mach three plus, exaggerated control movements are likely to cause dramatic, possibly catastrophic, changes in attitude. At the Blackbird's operating altitude, air densi-

The "A-11" announced by LBJ, which was in reality the AMI, later designated YF-12A. First publicity photos showed the YF-12s in their CIA (mostly natural metal, ala A-12) finishes. (USAF)

Kelly Johnson, head of Lockheed's advanced development projects (Skunk Works) during the development of the Blackbird. Johnson joined Lockheed in 1933 as a tool designer, and rose to the position of Chief Research Engineer by 1938. His famous projects include the P-38, F-80, F-104, U-2, and the Blackbird. He was photographed with the number three YF-12A shortly after it was announced to the public in 1964. (Lockheed)

Between the time the Blackbirds were publically announced in February, 1964 and their debut in September of the same year, they acquired the overall Blackpaint scheme which would ultimately cause them to be christened "Blackbird". (I have heard the assertion that they are actually dark Blue, but like everything else about the Blackbird, the actual specification is secret, and they certainly look Blacker than Black in person!) (USAF)

ty is less than 2% of sea level, necessitating larger control movements. Sitting fifty feet in front of the center of gravity, the pilot will be the last one to know if his inputs are correct. High performance is dependent upon an artificial Stability Augmentation System (SAS) which relieves the pilot of the constant pressure of balancing a 2,000 MPH see-saw. The Honeywell-designed SAS has proven to be one of the most reliable of the Blackbird's sub-systems, recording a 130,000 hour MTBF rate!

Honeywell also developed the Air Data Computer. The Air Data Computer compensates for the effects of high Mach number and gives accurate readings of altitude, vertical speed, and Mach number on it's triple-display digital indicator. (Because of the low air density at the Blackbird's operating altitude, the standard pressure instruments are unreliable.)

With skin temperatures ranging from 450 to over 1200 degrees Fahrenheit at cruise speeds, and the entire airframe soaking in these temperatures for extended periods of time, it was necessary to develop new fuels, hydraulic fluids, oil, sealants, insulating materials, and a whole host of related items. These temperatures immediately eliminated most coventional airframe fabricating materials and techniques. They also eliminated all but the toughest of titanium alloys. Over 93% of the basic structure of the Blackbird is titanium. At Mach 3 the skin reaches maximum temperature within 11 minutes, while the balance of the aircraft may take up to 35 minutes to reach steady state temps. Cooling is accomplished through radiation, which is the reason that Blackbirds are Black. The high emmisivity paint applied to Blackbirds radiates heat at almost three times the rate of natural metal. The JP-7 fuel provides a measure of cooling, though as the fuel load is burn-

Blended Forward wing (chine)

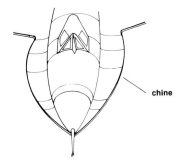

chine

A-12 with chine

A-12 with chine removed

ed down the fuselage suffers differential heating which causes the chines to be drawn downward. Fuel is used to cool some of the most sensitive components, notably the landing gear. Tires are inflated with nitrogen to maintain equal pressure throughout all flight regimes. The fuel used in Blackbirds is JP-7, which has such a high flash point that it must be ignited with a special chemical called TRI Ethyl Borane, (TEB).

The Blackbird does not use fuel bladders. The aircraft skin forms the upper and lower walls of the six fuel tanks, and even though they are resealed every 200 hours of flight time, the expansion and contraction of the airframe caused by heating and cooling results in some severe leakage. Since there is no evaporation of JP-7, the pools of fuel that collect under parked aircraft present little, if any, fire hazard. But even the high flash point of JP-7 might not withstand the skin temperatures of fuel tanks subjected to sustained Mach 3 flight. These temps reach close to 600 degrees and require nitrogen inerting of the fuel cells during flight.

The oil used in the J-58 engine is so heavy that is is virtually solid at temperatures below 86 degrees Fahrenheit. It has to be preheated before flight, at the rate of 1 hour per 10 degrees of heat required to get it up to 86 degrees. A special silicon-based instrument transducer librucant takes the place of grease on those items that require lubrication.

Special hydraulic fluid was developed to withstand the operating tempeatures of up to 650 degrees Fahrenheit. To prevent burning of this fluid, which would cause varnishing and ultimate failure of servos and valves, the fluid must be kept free of oxygen, both in systems and in the aircraft. This is done by pressurizing hydraulic systems and inerting with nitrogen. Special metal-to-metal sealings or metal O rings take the place of ordinary O rings.

The electrical connectors must be gold-plated to protect them from heat damage. Silver-zinc batteries that are used for emergency power have to be removed from the aircraft after each flight for recharging, which takes two days. These batteries are also pressurized with nitrogen to prevent explosions at high operating temps.

The cockpit of the Blackbird is seven times harder to cool than the cockpit of the X-15 was. The fuel supply is used for this, and the air conditioner keeps the cockpit temperature at an average 60 degrees in spite of outside cockpit wall temps of up to 400 degrees. Other problem areas caused by the high operating temperatures included fabricating parachutes that could be either protected from or resistant to the heat, ejection seat propellants that wouldn't cook off at high temps, and control cables that would maintain their strength at high temps. (The latter problem was solved with the use of Elgiloy, the high tensile strength alloy used in watch springs.) Special plastics had to be developed for the radome of the YF-12A, and developing reconnaissance systems that could "look" through the super-heated windows and air around their bays was a major problem on the A-12 and SR-71.

Crew escape at Mach 3 and 80,000 feet is acomplished through the use of a pressure suit, which provides enough protection to survive an ejection at speed and altitude. The suits are custom made for their owners and cost $100,000 per copy. (Gloves are manufactured in sets of three pair, at $6,000 per set.) The ejection system has been proven on several occasions, though none have been publically officially documented. Reportedly, the first loss of a Blackbird was during a Mach 3 test flight in which the forwad fuselage tank has been emptied because of a high rate of leakage. Entering a turn at Mach 3, the too-far aft CG caused a severe pitchup, resulting in a breakup of the airframe. The test pilot found himself outside the airplane as it disintegrated. He survived, thanks to the suit.

The cost and complexity of learning to machine the high strength Beta B-120 titanium alloy was staggering for it's day. In the early sixties, Lockheed was paying $119 per foot for titanium extrusions, and it was costing $19 per inch to machine them. In the process of this testing program 40,000 examples of a test part were manufactured in one month, with a loss of 95% of them.

The Blackbird's engines are Pratt and Whitney JT11D-20, whose military desgination is J-58. At Mach 3 plus, it is very nearly a perpetual motion machine, operating in afterburner at cruise and still with a low enough specific fuel consumption to allow a range of nearly 3,000 miles! This feat could only be accomplished if the inlet and ejector sections of the engine were developed to the point where they produced a significant amount of the

thrust. In order to accomplish this, the designers moved the engines out away from the fuselage and it's disruptive airflow. This created a violent yawing when power was lost at speed. The stability augmentation system automatically compensates for this yaw so quickly that the pilot often does not know which engine he has "lost". Power loss occurs when the inlet "unstarts".

Since jet engines will not run on supersonic air, it is necessary to slow the inlet air down before it reaches the compressor. This is accomplished by the movable spike in the inlet, and by a series of bypass doors just aft of the inlet. At mach 3 the shock wave is trapped inside the inlet by the spike position. If, for any reason, the shock is ejected from the inlet, an unstart occurs. This is similar to a compressor stall, and causes a dramatic loss of thrust. The Automatic Flight Control System compensates immediately, taking the necessary actions to reposition the shock.

Aerodynamics were not the only problem encountered by the Blackbird's designers. Temperatures of over 800 degrees at the inlets, 350 degrees at the fuel inlets, afterburner fuel nozzle temps of 600 degrees, and lubricant temperatures of up to 1,000 degrees combine.

YF-12A undergoing ground checks during the intitial flight test. Note that the YF-12s apparently were equipped with a different ejection seat than the SR-71. (Lockheed)

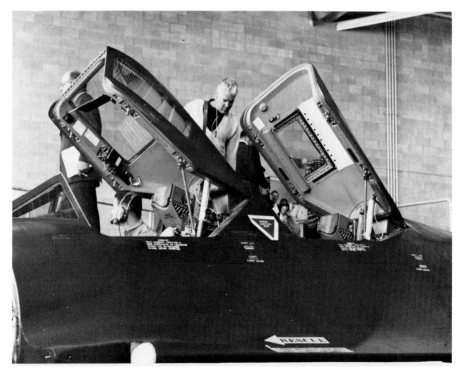

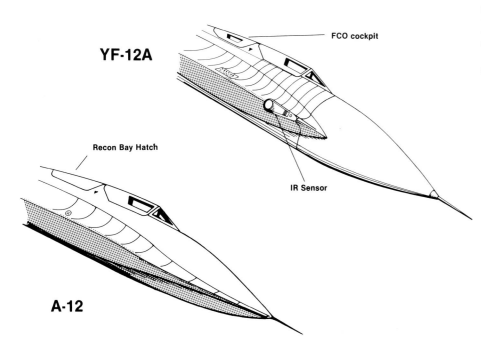

YF-12A

FCO cockpit

Recon Bay Hatch

IR Sensor

A-12

When the YF-12A Blackbirds were first shown to the public in September, 1964, 06934 and 06936 put on the flying display, while 06935 was on static display. They carried Air Defense Command badges on the port vertical tail, and Air Systems Command badges on the starboard vertical fin. Pods carried under nacelles contained cameras that were used to record missile launches. Landing gear retraction is necessarily rapid, since the Blackbird accelerates quickly to it's maximum gear transition speed of 300 knots. (Lockheed)

bined to create monumental problems for Pratt & Whitney engineers. (If you are becoming temperature-jaded, go take a look at the dial on your oven to ehance your appreciation of the problems the Blackbird's designers faced.) The operating temperatures encountered in the J-58 dictated all new parts, right down to the last screw.

A grest deal of the design work on the engines was verified in wind tunnel testing, but a significant amount could only be done in flight test. Temperatures created problems for the test instrumentation, which was not designed to withstand the operating environment of the J-58. A special water cooling system had to be designed and built just to obtain test data!

Fine tuning of the inlet system required the largest block of engine test time. Automatic scheduling of the spike and inlet doors are absolutely necessary to acheive maximum thrust with minimum drag. Operating forces of up to fourteen tons act on the spike, so the hydraulics required to move the spike forward and aft must be powerful *and* sensitive to maintain this delicate balance.

The engines, or the declining availability of them, may eventually retire the Blackbirds. J-58's have not been manufactured since the late sixties, and even though engines are completely disassembled and checked every 200 hours, they still wear out. Parts are beoming increasingly difficult to find, and engines are liable to sit for months awaiting parts before they can be put back into service. The Air Force does not advertise the number of operational SR-71s, but it is a safe bet that there are less than a dozen in service at any given time, and considering the lack of spares and the ever-longer in the tooth airframes, that figure will only continue to shrink.

The redesign of the nose shape to accomodate the YF-12A Fire Control System is obvious in this bottom view of the Fighter version of the Blackbird. (John Mallozzi)

YF-12A

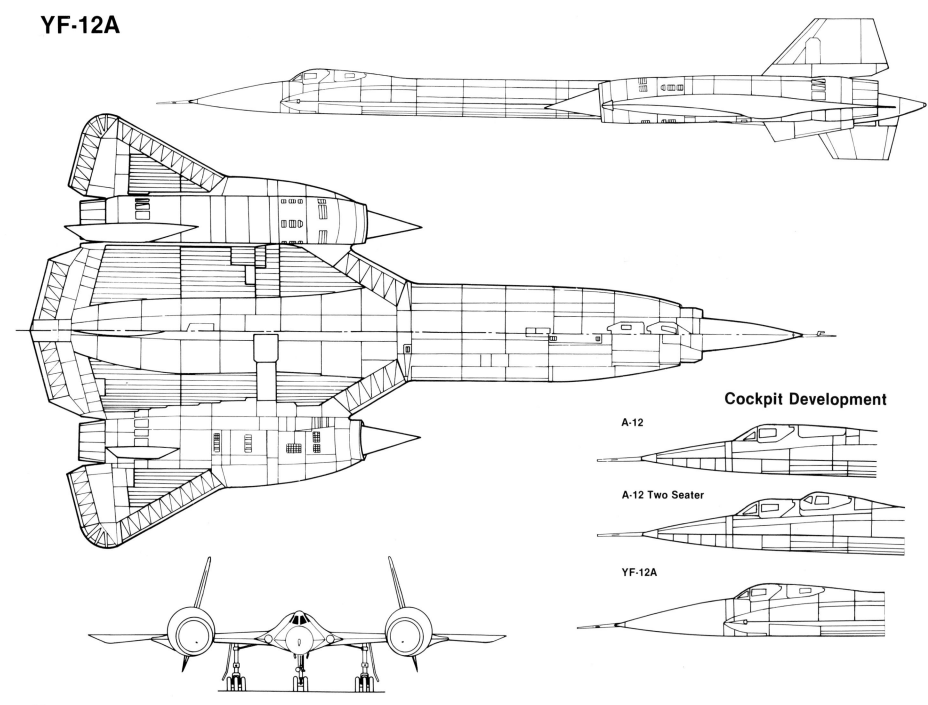

Cockpit Development

A-12

A-12 Two Seater

YF-12A

Yf-12A #06936 taxies in after a test flight. Note that the drag chute compartment doors are still open. White markings on undersides were to aid in calibration of record-run instrumentation during the record-setting flights of May 1, 1965. (Lockheed)

06935 gets away on a test flight. Note that the center ventral fin has begun to unfold as the gear begins it's retraction cycle. (Lockheed)

Final configuration of the chines on 06935. It is now displayed in the Air Force Museum. (John Andrews)

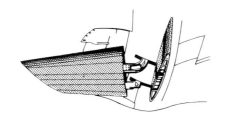

Folding Ventral Fin

For Ground Clearance Fin folded to port when landing gear was extended.

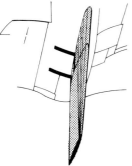

Fin folds down when landing gear retracts

Fire Control Officer's canopy and window on the YF-12A. (John Andrews)

YF-12A at Edwards AFB, 1964. Note open missile bay under port chine. The Long range ASG-18 radar used a combination of infrared and pulse Doppler to detect and track low flying targets. (Lockheed)

ASG-18 Fire Control Radar

YF-12A used a combination of long range radar and infrared search sensors along with a precision radar coupled to the infrared tracking system.

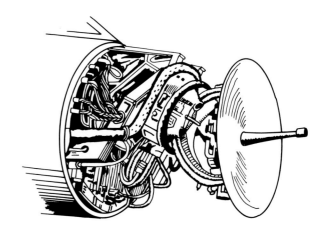

Range of the radar and infrared trackers was estimated at 200 to 300 miles when it was first shown, giving the YF-12 unparalelled ability to detect and destroy enemy aircraft. (Lockheed)

NASA's F-104 flew chase on the Blackbirds during the NASA YF-12 test program, which began in 1969. (Lockheed)

(Above right) YF-12A at the Air Force Flight Test Center, Edwards AFB in May, 1969. It is marked with the outstanding unit citation earned by the AirForce's YF-12 flight test team. Mission marks on nose are Blackbird silhouettes. (D. Kasulka via N. E. Taylor)

06935 at Edwards in 1966. (via Paul Stevens)

A-12　　　　**YF-12A**

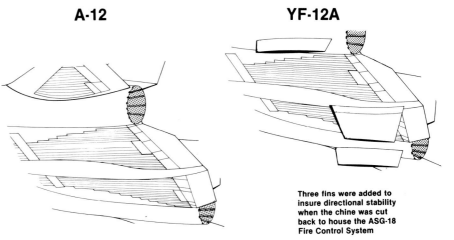

Three fins were added to insure directional stability when the chine was cut back to house the ASG-18 Fire Control System

(Above) Don Mallick was chief pilot at NASA's Dryden Flight Research Center at Edwards AFB during the YF-12 test flight program. In addition to his work with the Blackbirds, Mallick also was project pilot on the Lunar Landing Research Vehicle program, which led to the successful development of the LEM. He also flew the M-2 lifting body. (NASA)

(Right) 06935 during the NASA flight test program. White markings are to aid in calibration of tracking instrumentation during the flight test program. Note that it is sans the large center ventral fin. The fin broke loose on an earlier test flight, rupturing a fuel tank. (NASA)

(Below) A semi-revealing look at the innards of the Blackbird provided by this shot of 935 with some access panels removed. (NASA)

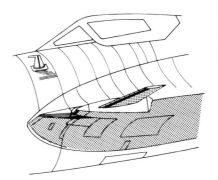

Small canards were tested on the YF-12s during the NASA test program.

(Above) The YF-12 undergoing extensive preflight preparations at Edwards in 1971. (NASA)

(Below) One of the primary areas investigated by NASA was the use of newer materials to combat the high temperatures encountered in sustained high speed flight. Among these materials were graphite/polymides that were fabricated for wing panels. NASA research led to new designs for high speed wind tunnels. The NASA C-77-4656 YF-12 model is shown in the tunnel at Lewis Research Center, Cleveland, Ohio. (NASA)

(Above) One of the most startling of NASA discoveries was the fact that, at Mach 3, 50% of the Blackbird's drag was generated by air vented out of the bypass doors. (NASA)

The last flight of 06935 brought it to Wright Patterson AFB and the Air Force Museum. It was a traffic-stopping event! (Lockheed)

The Blackbird is displayed after its arrival at the Air Force Museum with another of Kelly Johnson's designs, the F-80 Shooting Star, America's first operational jet fighter. (David Menard)

All Moving Vertical Stabilizer

Maximum movement of ± 20 degrees

The abrupt ending of the chines of the YF-12A are especially evident in this photo. 06934 and 36 were both destroyed in crashes, leaving 935 as the sole surviving YF-12A. (NASA)

D-21 DRONE

Very few people were aware that the Lockheed GTD-21 Drone even existed until several examples showed up at USAF's military aircraft storage and disposition center at Davis-Monthan AFB in late 1976. It was an impromptu retirement party, but the fact that the D-21's were escorted to their retirement home by armed guards spoke volumes for the secret nature of their operational life.

It wasn't long before the D-21s were spotted languishing in the Arizona sun, more than slightly incongruous among the T-34s and T-28s in neighboring parking areas. Pictures were taken, questions were asked, and various versions of what they were, what they did, where they came from, and how many were built began to emerge. In it's October 31, 1977 issue, Aviation Week & Space Technology quoted an "Official" as saying "that the drone was conceived as a subscale prototype for the initial proof-of-concept flight testing of design features that were applied to the A-11." AW&ST also revealed that 38 D-21's had been built, in the time frame 1964-1967, and that they had performed the interim strategic reconnaissance mission, while the SR-71 was becoming operational. They asserted that the drone was carried aloft semi-submerged in the belly of the A-11/YF-12A, then released at altitude and speed.

Whether the drone was indeed conceived as a proof-of-concept model for the Blackbird may be open to speculation. And as long as we are speculating, is it possible tha the D-21 was conceived and designed to overfly sensitive areas, thus circumventing Ike's promise to stop manned overflights of the USSR? It is now known that the drone was carried atop the rear fuselage of the A-12, and that it's flight test period coincided with that of the A-12.

No performance figures were ever officially released for the D-21, but it has been assumed that it's performance may approach the hypersonic regime, at altitudes in excess of 100,000 feet, with a range of 1,250 miles. No information has been made available concerning the engine of the D-21, but it is evident, from the design features of the D-21, that it may be a scaled down version of the J-58, with one notable exception. It has been assumed that the D-21's engine is closer to a pure ramjet, and that it could only be started at high mach numbers. The D-21's in storage at Davis-Monthan bear no national markings, and the few maintenance markings are stenciled in small Red letters, making them all but

A-12 #06940 with the D-21 Drone. Release of the drone occured at high speed, and was expedited by the use of ballistic charges. (Reportedly, the drone engine was more ram-jet than turbo-jet, and could not be started at less than the high Mach numbers generated by the Blackbird.) The normal recon bay behind the cockpit of the A-12 was occupied by the drone Launch Control Officer when the drone was carried. One of the A-12 losses was rumored to have occured as a result of one of these missions, when the ballistic separation of the two forced the A-12 to pitch up into the drone after it had been launched. (USAF)

invisible at distance. The reconnaissance bays are in the belly of the drone, just ahead of the wing crank line. Naturally, no information has been made available as to the type of equipment carried, and no pictures taken by the D-21 have ever been released under it's byline. "Remove Before Flight" tags attached to the spike boom contained three digit numbers ranging from 503 to 539, and the aircraft designation GTD-21B.

Presumably, the construction of the D-21 is similar to that of the Blackbird, with titanium as the principle material in the airframe. Those now in storage are Black.

It is curious that in all the semi-classified briefings and scientific symposiums of the Blackbird, the drone has been almost totally ignored. It is also curious that, though the Air Force stated that the D-21 was on "retired reserve" from 1968 to 1976, it's official retirement to Davis-Monthan coincided almost exactly with the retirement of the A-12s to Palmdale. To paraphrase a famous line; "Who are those guys, and what are them things?"

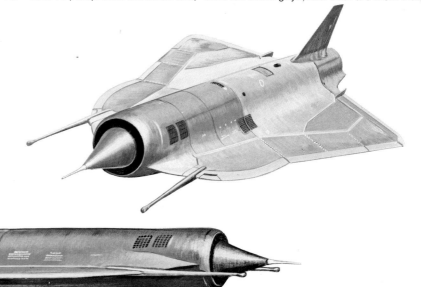

"Blackbird vs. Foxbat"

Soviet development of the Mig-25 has been attributed at various times to the threat posed by either the B-70 Valkyrie, or to the Blackbird. Cancellation of the Valkyrie has also been attributed to the threat posed by the Mig-25, though that is doubtful, since the Mig-25 was not seen publicly until 1967, and it's capabilities were not known for several years after that. A more likely reason for cancellation of the B-70 was the cost of producing it, compared with the cost of a whole battery of SAMs, which might be expected to have a better than even chance of bringing the B-70 down. Even after the B-70 was cancelled, development and production of the Foxbat went forward. The Blackbird posed a much more formidable threat, with it's demonstrated ability to sustain cruise speeds above Mach three at over 80,000 feet.

The Mig-25 Foxbat has presented as much an enigmatic image as the Blackbird, at times being reported as invincible, and at other times being dismissed as practically prehistoric in it's approach to high speed and altitude flight. Naturally, it is to the advantage of the anti-military press to derogate the threat posed by the Mig-25, and they were quick to seize upon the fact that it does not approach the sophistication of the Blackbird, even though it was developed in the same time period. Titanium is used sparingly in the Mig-25, (for the most part, only on leading edges of wings and tail) and it's arc-welded surfaces do look crude. It's engines are powerful, but it's airframe is relatively straightforward, and does not contribute to enhanced high speed performance as the Blackbird's does.

On the other hand, the pro-military press feels the need to enhance the threat posed by the Mig-25, and may attach more significance to it's design sophistication than is warranted. After all, without the spur of a clear and imminent danger, the American People have shown a great deal of reluctance to invest in defense.

Regardless of the capabilities of the Mig-25, the significant fact of it's development is in it's operational deployment. The Soviets have built over 400 Foxbats, and are continuing to develop it as an advanced interceptor. There have been A,B,C,D, and now MP versions of the Foxbat. The only version western experts have had a chance to examine in detail is the A, delivered courtesy of Lieutenant Viktor Belenko in 1976. A great deal was made of it's nickel steel construction, and it's vacuum tube avionics. Belenko, in his biography, states that SR-71's flew off the coast of Russia, "taunting and toying with Mig-25s sent up to intercept them, scooting up to altitudes the Soviet planes could not reach, and circling leisurely above them, or dashing off at speeds the Russians could not match." According to Belenko, the Mig-25 pilots were forbidden to exceed Mach 2.5, and he maintained that the Foxbat could not safely exceed 2.8. When told that Mig-25's had been clocked at Mach 3.2 on overflights of Israel, he said that the engines had been completely destroyed by these speeds, and that the pilots had been lucky to live through the experience. Combat radius was limited to 186 miles in combat situation. (Using afterburner and carrying a full load of missiles.) With a load of two Acrid missiles, the Foxbat could reach 78,000 feet, but with it's full complement of four missiles, it was limited to 68,900 feet. Since the SR-71 cruises faster than the top speed of these missiles, there was no chance of a tail-chase interception, and apparently the Foxbat's radar and fire control system was not sophisticated enough to solve the problems of a head-on intercept at closing speeds that would exceed Mach 5.

With a full load of fuel and missiles, the Foxbat is limited to 2.2 Gs. Lightly loaded, it is limited to 5 Gs. The early interceptor models possessed the world's most powerful radar, which is virtually jam-proof. It does not have look-down, shoot-down capability, and cannot track targets below about 2,000 feet.

The Mig-25, in it's earlier versions, was certainly not the technological threat that most American analysts had thought it to be. But it was a remarkable engineering feat, in that

The Second YF-12A, equipped with a Coldwall experiment to study effects of aerodynamic heating on a cylinder cooled with gaseious nitrogen. (Large cylinder under fuselage) It has also been fitted with the camera pods originally installed on 06934 to record missile firings. The SR-71 prototype (sometimes referred to as the YF-12C) is flying chase. During one test flight, these two aircraft experienced nearly simultaneous unstarts. The YF-12 actually lost both engines and had to relight them at lower altitude. (NASA)

the Soviets had gotten the most of a very primitive design. It could not be compared to the Blackbird in terms of design sophistication or innovation. But more importantly, it proved the Russian determination to achieve at least a rough parity with the west, and to surpass the west if only in terms of sheer force of numbers. In that context, the Foxbat is a very clear and present danger, for it is still in production while the Blackbird is in the twilight of it's career with no successor on the visible horizon.

SR-71 Blackbird

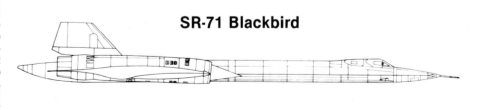

MiG 25 Foxbat

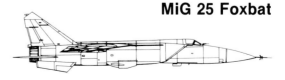

The SR-71 Blackbird prototype in flight over the snowcapped Sierra Mountains. The YF-12 test program was finishing as the SR-71 was becoming operational. (NASA)

SR-71A serial number 64-17964 taxies away from the special hangars (built for exclusive use of the Blackbirds) at Beale AFB for a training mission during March of 1980. The camera nose is fitted, with cameras installed. (C.B. Mayer)

SR-71A about to plug into a KC-135Q tanker. Blackbird tankers are fitted with a special interphone link in the refuelling boom, enabling the boom operator and the SR-71 pilot to communicate on a secure link and maintain radio silence. (USAF)

The tail of operational 17955, an SR-71A, which carries the famed "skunk."

Operational SR-71A 17967 flew out of Kadena.

06934 was the first of four prototypes in the YF-12A program.

"Rapid Rabbit" was the name given to 17978

17976 carried the wing emblem of the 9th SRW.

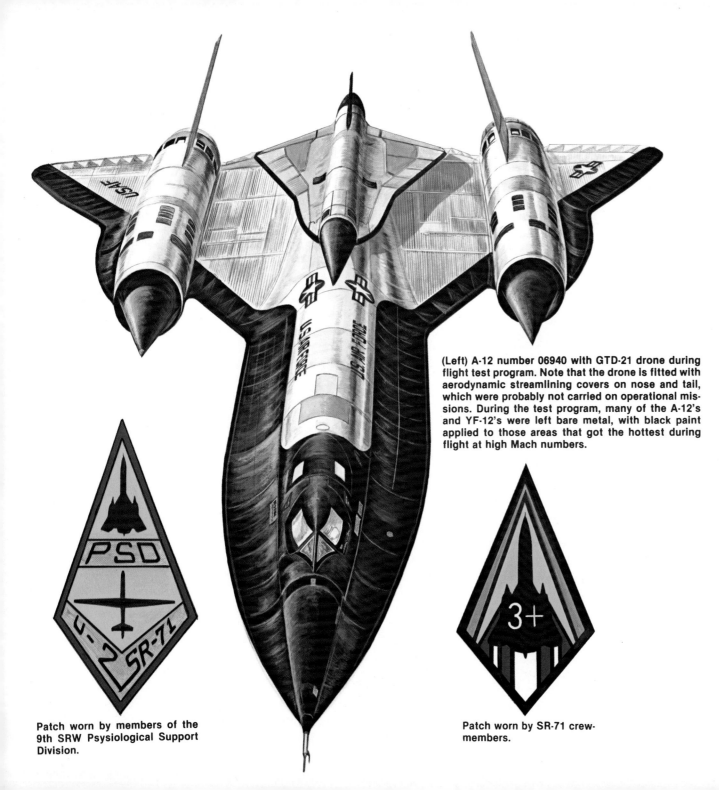

(Left) A-12 number 06940 with GTD-21 drone during flight test program. Note that the drone is fitted with aerodynamic streamlining covers on nose and tail, which were probably not carried on operational missions. During the test program, many of the A-12's and YF-12's were left bare metal, with black paint applied to those areas that got the hottest during flight at high Mach numbers.

Patch worn by members of the 9th SRW Psysiological Support Division.

Patch worn by SR-71 crewmembers.

06935 was used by NASA for high speed flight experiments.

17974

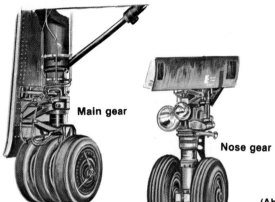

Main gear

Nose gear

Emblem of the 1st Strategic Reconnaissance Squadron, worn by crews on their flight suits.

(Above) Provisional engine starter cart used twin Buick V-8's (unmuffled) to provide starting power to the SR-71's J-58's prior to installation of a permanent starting system in the hangers at Beale.

(Below)*Ichi Ban*, SR-71 974, landing at Beale, probably in the late 60's or early 70's.(USAF)

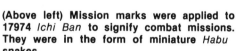

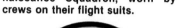

(Above left) Mission marks were applied to 17974 *Ichi Ban* to signify combat missions. They were in the form of miniature *Habu* snakes.

(Left) SR-71 crewman in full pressure suit, seated in SR-71 ejection seat, next to *HABU* patch. Nickname given the Blackbird by Okinawans who saw a similarity between the SR-71 and the deadly native Habu snake, the patch is awarded to SR-71 crew after they fly their first operational mission.

Cockpit area of 17964. (C.B. Mayer)

Rear Fuselage Development

YF-12A

SR-71A

A glimpse of the special equipment in the rear cockpit of the SR-71A is provided by this over-the-shoulder view of 17958 at Beale AFB. (USAF via C.B. Mayer)

BLACKBIRD FACTS AND FIGURES

YF-12A
Length: (excluding nose probe) 101.66 feet. **Span:** 55.62 feet, **Height:** 18.38 feet, **Fuselage ventral fin Area,** M2: 6.735, **Chords:** root 13.7' tip 8.5', **Nacelle ventral fin Area,** M2: 2.044, **Chords: root 13.93' tip 10.7'.**

SR-71A:
Length: (excluding nose probe) 103.876 feet. **Length of nose probe:** 4'11'', **Span:** 55.62 feet, **Height:** 18'6'', **Wing area:** 1795.00 square feet, **Aspect ratio:** 1.939, **Root chord:** 60.533 feet, **Tip chord:** 0.00, **Dihedral:** 0 degrees, **Sweep:** 52.629 degrees, **Inboard elevon area:** 39.00 square feet, **Outboard elevon area:** 52.50 square feet, **Vertical tail total area:** 150.76 square feet, **Movable tail area:** 70.24 square feet, **Root chord:** 14.803 feet, **Tip chord:** 7.833 feet, **Fuselage diameter:** 5.33 feet, **Maximun take-off weight:** 170,000 lbs. (estimated), **Empty Weight:** 60,000 lbs. (estimated), **Equipment:** Wide variety of specialized reconnaissance sensors including, but not limited to, high resolution cameras, side-looking radar, and IR photography equipment. Recon bays are configured to accomodate various combinations of recon packages, depending on particular mission requirements. **Max speed:** Classified (see records section), **Max altitude:** Classified (see records section). **(Note:** Janes quotes a max dash speed of 2,350MPH and a max long range cruise of 1,980MPH, but these figures are not officially verified.)

YF-12A

SR-71A

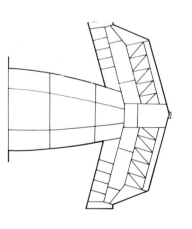

YF-12A

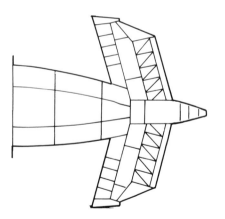

SR-71A

SR-71A

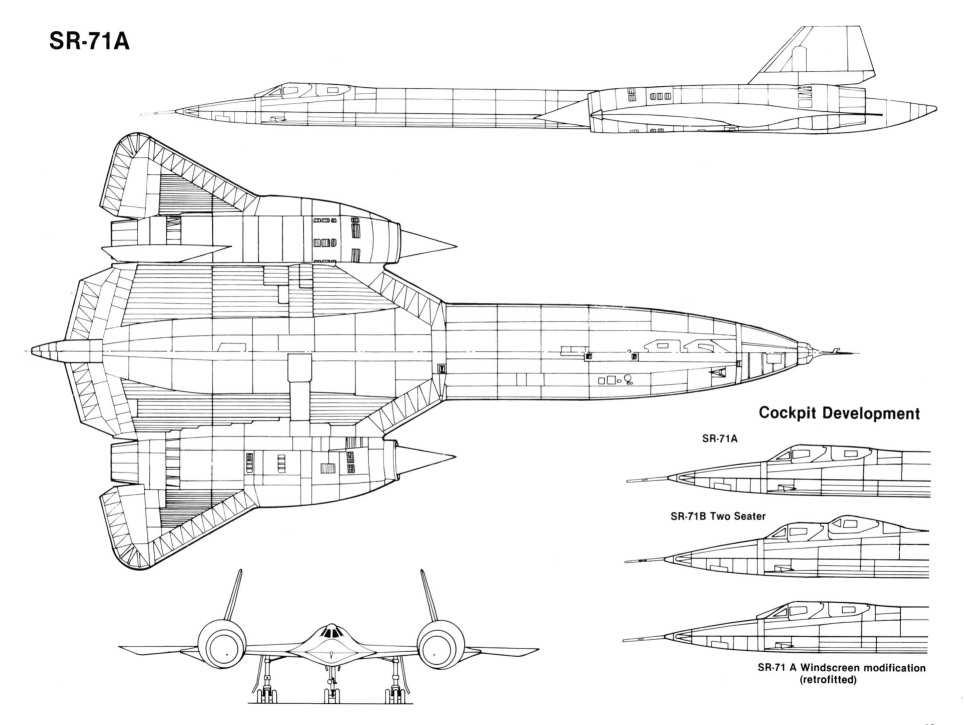

Cockpit Development

SR-71A

SR-71B Two Seater

SR-71 A Windscreen modification (retrofitted)

29

SR-71A 17975 being towed to the airshow line at Norton AFB, CA with a VIP in the cockpit. (Ted Carlson)

Note single canopy opening piston and the smooth line of the chine. (Ted Carlson)

Canopy of 17964. These windows will reach temperatures of up to 400 degrees Fahrenheit in Mach 3 flight, enabling crews to heat the tube food carried on operational missions by holding it against the window for a short period. (Ted Carlson)

ECM Antenna Dents

Latest modification to the nose of the SR-71 interrupts the smooth line of the chines with ECM "dents". (C.B. Mayer)

Over-the-shoulder view of the panel of the cockpit of the SR-71A simulator. (USAF via James Goodall)

(right) Possible look of concern on the face of this pilot may have something to do with the fact that he is about to fly 17958, an aircraft with a reputation for erratic behaviour, though at least one crew reports having no problems with this particular aircraft. (USAF via C.B. Mayer)

The suit worn by SR-71 crewmen is identical to that now used in the Space Shuttle. It is the principle protection in the event of an ejection at high Mach and altitude, and has been proven in several cases to be effective. (Author)

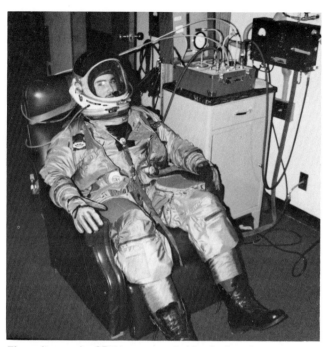

The Lockheed ejection set used in the SR-71. (Author)

FLYING THE BLACKBIRD

The broad lifting area provided by the double delta design of the Blackbird is evident, as is the leading edge camber of the outer wing panels. (USAF)

It is probably the most exclusive fraternity of airmen in the world today, with fewer members than the astronaut corps. In the whole history of Blackbird operations probably less than one hundred pilots have checked out in the three variants of the Blackbird. Since the number of SR-71s is classified, the current number of operational crews is unavailable, but Air Force sources have indicated that there are less than "a couple of dozen" crews.

SR-71 crews are selected from hundreds of volunteers annually. As the only flying assignment in the Air Force which cannot be allocated by the omnipotent computer, the SR-71 assignment generates competition for it's limited number of slots. Some of the most upwardly mobile career officers in the Air Force have made flying the SR-71 one of the most interesting milestones in outstanding careers. Of the original 57 pilots and RSOs when the 9th Strategic Reconnaissance Wing (SRW) was formed in 1966, 25 had been promoted to Colonel, 3 to Brigadier General, 4 to Major General, and 1 to Lieutenant General as of 1980.

Qualifications and the selection process are remarkably similar to those used to choose the Thunderbirds. An applicant must have at least 1500 hours of jet time, and be able to pass the rigorous Aerospace Research Pilot School physical examination. (The same exam given to astronaut applicants.) If these qualifications are met, the volunteer's service record is given a thorough going-over by the 9th SRW's selection board, whose members are all experienced SR-71 pilots and/or RSOs. Those judged to be the most qualified for the singularly demanding job of SR-71 operations are invited to Beale AFB for a one week round of personal interviews, simulator rides, and flights in the T-38. (The T-38 has sub-sonic handling qualities that closely approximate those of the SR-71, and Blackbird pilots fly the Talon on a regular basis to maintain proficiency.) The wing will eventually accept about 10% of the original applicants for training. The profile of the average SR-71 crewman reads something like this: 33 years old, 2500 hours total jet time,

rank of major, and a better than average ability to refrain from talking about his job to all but his contemporaries.

It is an elite group, but unlike the Thunderbirds or the astronauts, it is not a well-publicised profession. The rewards of the SR-71 crewman are personal satisfaction in a difficult job well done. While most of the rest of the Air Force devotes it's time to training for the date it might have to go to war, the Strategic Reconnaissance crew performs before a live audience on a day-to-day basis. Once an SR-71 crew is certified "mission capable", there are no more dry runs. One mistake could mean an international incident that might possibly cost the crew their lives at worst, and embarrass the United States at best.

One of the crews flying the SR-71 out of Beale AFB in early 1982 was made up of pilot Major Gil Bertelson and RSO Major Frank Stampf. Gil Bertelson's first operational assignment was in Training Command, as a T-37 Instructor Pilot. He went from T-37's to the F-111, flying the F model at Mountain Home AFB and RAF Lakenheath, and the A model in Thailand. Frank Stampf accumulated 1600 hours in the RF-4 before being accepted for SR-71 training in 1979. Their experience is typical of most of the SR-71 crews flying today.

Gil and Frank were paired up as crew shortly after being notified of their acceptance into the program. Crew integrity is one of the rigid rules of Blackbird operations. The aircraft and avionics systems are so sophisticated that it requires a great deal of crew coordination to operate them successfully. For that reason, crews are never broken up for operational missions, and most crews go through the entire training and operational flying cycle together. I asked them to describe the SR-71 training program.

Gil: *The pilot probably has 85 to 100 hours, minimum, of simulator time before he gets into the airplane. The RSO would probably have about 20 hours more in the simulator because he doesn't get into the airplane until we are completely through with the 'Initial Qual' portion of the simulator program. We have* a series of thirteen 'Initial Qual Sims'. These are four hours long, and are preceded by familiarization 'sims' for that phase. The pilot will have ten of these periods before he gets into the airplane, while the RSO will have all thirteen before he flies. There are Instructor Pilots and RSOs operating the simulator for both 'fams' and 'qual-sims' The program calls for the pilot to have at least five initial 'qual' rides in the B model, with the fifth being the check ride. As I recall, I had six or seven, due to weather and airplane problems that caused us to shorten one mission and to abort another. At that point we begin the Mission Qualification phase. I flew MQ-1 and MQ-2 with an experienced RSO, and Frank flew the same missions with an experienced pilot. We were teamed up on MQ-3, and flew the balance of our training missions together.

Earlier, I had heard that crews had to have at least 60 hours before they were considered mission-ready. I asked Gil how much time they would have beginning MQ-3.

Gil: *The B model rides probably average 3 to 3½ hours each, so with the IQ rides and MQ-1 and 2, I might have up to 30 hours. Frank would probably only have 7 or 8.*

Frank: *The 60 hour figure is reached at about the completion of MQ-6, which is when the wing normally plans to certify you mission ready. This is not a hard and fast figure, and really has more to do with administrative classification of aircrews. It is not an experience plateau, since you are really not ready to fly operational missions at this point, though the wing might certify you mission ready.*

Gil: *We continue to fly training missions here to build time. The wing has a requirement that you have at least 100 hours before you go on your first TDY. That is when you are mission ready for real.*

Frank: *The instruction that we get in the initial qualification phase is very, very intensive. During our simulator training, we get a chance to experience everything that has ever happened to the airplane, and anything that computer projections say could happen to the airplane under various sets of circumstances. Almost every crew member, to a man, that I have talked to, while not being bored with their first ride in the airplane, would say that it (their first flight) was a piece of cake...just because of the thorough wringing-out we get in the simulator. It*

gives you a very comfortable feeling when you get into the cockpit for the first time.

Even after all that training, there comes a time when someone has to certify that the new crew is indeed mission ready. In tactical aircraft, an instructor pilot would fly wing on the new pilot, evaluating his performance during the flight. While it would not be impossible to put up a formation of Blackbirds, there is a much more accurate and economical method of checking both new crews, and operational crews during their annual "stan-eval" ride.

Frank: *After we have been flying together for a certain amount of time, we come to a point in the training program when we are ready for our final check-ride. After a final emergency procedures check in the simulator, we will go fly a normal training mission, then when we return, the evaluation board will pull the tapes from the Mission Recorder System, (an on-board computer that monitors and records all phases of flight, including operation of aircraft systems, and altitude, speed, and track.) and evaluate our performance. The pilot evaluator will be looking at all the parameters that Gil maintained during climb, cruise, and descent. The RSO will be looking at me for sensor operation, navigation computer operation, and cross track variance from our mission profile. All those parameters can be read off the mission tapes, and they are used to give us our check rides.*

Both Gil and Frank had been in tactical aircraft that regularly flew low-level high speed missions. These are missions in which the adrenal flow can be expected to attain a high rate, and which demand a great deal of concentration. I asked them to compare the SR-71 mission with the mission of the RF-4 and F-111s that they had been flying.

Gil: *When I was in the F-111, I can recall thinking that the SR mission could not possibly be as demanding as the 111. I remember thinking: Well, you take off, get very high, fly very fast, then come down...nothin' to it. Then I got into the SR program and found out how wrong I had been. I think there are TIMES when the low-level, high-speed mission is perhaps more intense, but our mission is basically intense from take-off until landing. The SR mission is more demanding,*

17950 was last seen at Beale in 1970. (Lockheed)

The crew chief waves an SR-71 out of it's individual shelter at Beale AFB. In order to conceal the number of SR-71s, the 9th SRW keeps most of the hangars closed, and may open empty hangars, or hangars with aircraft in them at random. It is a shell game that keeps casual observers wondering how many and where. (USAF)

With a light fuel load, the SR-71's 30,000lb plus thrust J-58 engines allow it to accelerate quickly to a liftoff speed of approximately 200 knots. (USAF)

Once the crew is fitted with their pressure suits, they need portable air conditioning units to maintain comfortable body temperatures until they are plugged into the aircraft. (USAF)

both physically and mentally. From a physical standpoint, you are wearing the pressure suit, which is another 40 pounds, and you are on 100% oxygen from the time you climb into the airplane until you shut it down. But more than that, I feel very, very mentally drained when I come home from a mission, because of the pressure to maintain very exact parameters throughout the flight. You don't have the luxury of looking outside very much either, so the total aspect of the mission is one that requires complete concentration.

Frank: *Just to expand on that a little...even if you take the pressure suit out of that equation...take the real life flying out, during the latter phase of our training, when we would spend 3½ to 4 hours in the simulator, with an hour or more of briefing prior to climbing into the box, then get hit with multiple emergencies, from the time you got in, until the time you got out, with all kinds of judgemental problems thrown at you constantly...even knowing you weren't going to crash and die if you didn't solve them correctly...why, we crawled out of there looking like a couple of whipped puppies! I can never remember feeling pressure like that in any other aircraft or simulator.*

I asked them if that was due to the fact that this training was more rigorous than normal tactical airplane drivers receive, or were there really that many more things to go wrong, or were they just that much more careful because of the scarcity and expense of the SR-71s?

Gil: *I think there is less margin for error in the environment that we fly in, so the training is more intense. In any other airplane you can take a fifteen or twenty degree heading change for 30 seconds and it doesn't do anything. Thirty seconds of that kind of heading change in the SR-71, depending upon what part of the world you're flying in, and you could find yourself on the front pages of the newspapers. It requires constant vigilance, regardless of whatever else may be going on in the airplane. The black line is the primary function of the aircrew.* (authors note: The 'black line' refers to a line drawn on a map for navigational reference, and is used in this context to describe a plotted flightpath over the surface of the the earth.) *Assuming that something has gone radically wrong, until such time as you can pick your abort base and safely get down from speed and altitude, you have to concentrate on flying that black line. All missions, operational or training are flown with the same attitude. You never get a chance to relax and sit back for five minutes...that time just never comes. In the F-4 or F-111, or any other aircraft, at some point you probably get the chance to sit back, fat, dumb, and happy for fifteen minutes or so...even if you are faced* with a letdown into 300 foot ceilings and a mile visibility at the home drome. You never get that chance with the SR-71.

Frank: *There are different phases of the mission, where it may be busier for one or the other of us. That is one of the reasons we have such extensive simulator training. It does a great deal to help us to develop close crew coordination. Gil will sense when I am very busy in the back, and rather than ask me to read a checklist, he will take that over and complete it himself. Conversely, when he is very busy I will try to take some of the load off his shoulders. The goal of a crew coordination is to even out the workload. An example of this is in the refuelling portion of the mission. It's my job to navigate us to the tanker on time and it gets very busy in the back during that time. Once we come up on the tanker, Gil will be working hard to complete the refuelling, particularly if there is turbulence, or if it's a hot day, and power limitations require him to light one of the burners to stay on the boom. If we are in the weather, he might even have the sensation of being inverted as we get bounced around and varying degrees of vertigo set in. It's up to me to monitor the instruments and help him out with fuel transfer figures, etc.*

In response to my question regarding the stability of the SR, Gil had this to say:

Except when you get into turbulence, it is relatively stable. But because of the long fuselage, you can get some pretty hairy diving board effects in turbulence. Another thing that affects stability is the placement of the engines as far apart as they are. When we are on the tanker, or making an instrument approach...any time fine throttle adjustments are necessary to effect immediate heading changes...you can get a lot of assymetrical thrust if the nozzles are not synched up just right.

It sounds as if the SR-71 is a real handful, but when asked if it was a difficult airplane to fly, Gil said:

Not really. Subsonic, it feels like a big, heavy airplane, and you have to horse the stick around a bit to get the airplane to move. Supersonically, it's not uncomfortable to hand-fly the airplane, but it does require a lot of attention to detail. The basic figures you work with...you take one degree of pitch change times your mach number, and that will equal your VVI (vertical velocity) change. For instance, if you're at mach three and you make a one degree pitch change, that will translate into an immediate 3,000 foot per minute climb or dive. That is not something you want to have at those speeds. The control inputs have to be very, very minute. On a check ride in the B model, we will typically hand-fly over 75% of the mission. As a matter of fact, on my last check ride, we never did engage the autopilot. That requires a lot of hard work, and it's obviously a lot easier for the pilot to turn on the autopilot, then just sit there and 'tweak' the system to maintain speed and altitude. As long as the system is running reasonably well, it is not difficult to fly the airplane, just intense. The simulator can, and has, shown us all the potentials for disaster when things are not running well. A few sessions like that in the simulator are enough to insure that concentration is maintained in the airplane.

The Blackbird is not your typical "kick the tires, light the fires, and let's go fly" type of airplane. Another Air Force source quoted a figure of $50,000 every time they start one up, so the missions are carefully planned. The mission planning is done the day prior to the mission. Crews will study film strips of the mission route, which include all checkpoints, and areas to be surveyed by the SR-71's sensors. The same film strips will be used in the moving map display in the cockpit. Once the route is decided upon, a tape will be used to program the SR's astro-inertial navigation computer.

On mission day, the crew eats a high-protein, low-residue breakfast before suiting up in their individual pressure suits. They are aided in donning of these very expensive custom-tailored portable environments by members of the 9 SRW's Physiological Support Division, which also supports the U-2 troops. With the suits on, the crew maintains a comfortable body temperature with portable air conditioning units until they are plugged into the airplane. They will be in the airplane, breathing 100% oxygen for at least 30 minutes prior to take-off in order to eliminate nitrogen from their systems and forestall the possibility of

17953 is one of the SR-71s lost. It took part in the SR-71 test program. (Note unit citation on tail and cross on nacelle) (Via Dave Menard)

decompression sickness at altitude.

Take off roll in the SR-71 will be about 4,400 feet, depending upon the fuel load, and lift-off speed will be 200-210 knots. The Blackbird accelerates quickly, and the pilot must exercise caution in order to preclue exceeding the 300 knot landing gear extension limit. Normal sub-sonic climb speed is 400 knots or 0.9 Mach. If an aerial refuelling is included in the mission profile, it will usually take place at 25,000 to 28,000 feet.

Acceleration to cruise speed and altitude will begin over a sparsely populated area to preclude sonic boom complaints. If the mission is hand flown, the pilot may perform a "dipsy" manuever to take the Blackbird through the transonic regime quickly, since that is the speed range in which the most drag is encountered. This requires a momentary leveling off to accelerate quickly through the mach before pulling the nose up and continuing the climb to altitude. If the acceleration and climb is accomplished on autopilot, the autopilot will be engaged in KEAS (Knots Equivalent Air Speed) mode, which follows a programmed Mach increase schedule until cruise speed and altitude is reached. In either case, manuevers are avoided during this phase of the flight, since fuel flow is highest during accel, and mission effectiveness often depends upon efficient management of fuel resources.

Once cruising altitude and Mach number are reached, the throttles are retarded to minimum afterburner, and the magic begins. The engines literally become little more than air-ingesters, with the inlets actually providing up to 60% of the thrust needed for Mach three-plus flight. The exhaust provides from 20% to 30% of the thrust.

It is a system that is at the very forefront of technology, even twenty years after it first flew! It operates on tight-rope tolerances, and must be closely monitored by the crew. So, while they never operate in actual instrument conditions at their operational altitudes, the crew is probably on instruments nearly all of the time. There is little reason for the crew to look outside the airplane in any case, since they are not likely to encounter much in the way of conflicting traffic. One exception to this might be the numerous weather balloons sent aloft. They present a real danger to SR crews, since the chances of avoiding one, if you were on a collision course, would be slim. Even if you saw the balloon well in advance, the problems of spatial relation, especially at high altitude where visual references are diminished greatly, might preclude your taking the correct evasive action. And any evasive action that was taken abruptly might get you into more trouble than no action at all.

The SR-71 is equipped with a three-axis, eight channel Stability Augmentation System (SAS) that senses, and compensates for the inherent instability of the Blackbird. I asked Gil and Frank how reliable the SAS was.

Gil: *We have never had a SAS problem. We have had a couple of potential problems with it, but have always been able to reset it and press on with the mission. I don't know that I have heard of anyone recently that has had a SAS problem that has affected a mission.*

I wondered if the Blackbird were capable of being flown at speed and altitude without the SAS system.

GIL: *Yes, it's a trick, but it can be done. It is really a question of the pilot's ability to maintain all the optimum parameters at this point.* (This was confirmed by NASA studies done at Langley Research Center in simulators. Highly experienced pilots were able to maintain assigned altitudes ±500 feet only 20% of the time at Mach 3.0 without the SAS.)

One of the most dramatic occurences in Mach 3 cruise flight is the expulsion of the supersonic shock wave from the engine inlet. This causes an "unstart", which is similar to a compressor stall. The system has been refined to such a high degree of reliability that unstarts are now a rarity. If an unstart should occur, the SAS would take immediate (within milliseconds) corrective action to counter the adverse yaw, while the inlets and spike were automatically being reprogrammed to recapture the shock wave within the inlet. Nevertheless, an unstart is a violent event, hearalded by a series of shuddering bangs, and head-snapping yaws. Crews have returned from unstart-punctuated missions with the heavy, tinted visor on their helmets cracked from contact with the cockpit walls caused by this snapping yaw. One pilot described an unstart as"...like being in a trainwreck!"

The question of just how fast the SR-71 will go, and how high it can fly is one that will be speculated upon by interested observers until official revelation of those numbers is forthcoming. In the meantime, it is interesting to note that the operational crews, though they certainly have a better idea of what these figures might be than most, probably don't know either just how high or how fast their airplane will fly. I nibbled at the edges of this question by speculating that it might be true that speed of the Blackbird might only be limited by the structural integrity of the engines and airframe. If you just put the throttles to the stops, would it be possible to exceed the redline of the airplane? **Gil:** *Yes, I would think you could, given the right set of conditions, but that's purely conjecture.* **Frank:** *You're talking to an operational, rather than a flight test crew. Our missions are very carefully planned and programmed, and we fly a very precise profile, so we never have the opportunity to do that. Strange as it may seem, we, as crews, are really not briefed on all that the airplane is capable of doing. We go through a very extensive academic program, but we are never in the position of just going out someday to see what the airplane will do. We are given an operational limitation on Mach and altitude, and we don't exceed it.*

Decelleration and descent are accomplished within a more rigid profile than the climb to altitude. Once the decel/descent is begun, throttle schedule is locked in until reaching Mach 1.3. At that point, the crew can adjust the descent profile. When flying within positive control airspace, it is imperative that the air traffic controllers understand the special circumstances of the SR-71 operation, and plan to integrate the Blackbird into their traffic flow within the parameters of the SR's operational limitations. This was the subject of an interesting anecdote.

Frank: *Anyone who flies gets tired of hearing the term 'stand by'. The controllers often are busy with something else, and are unable to respond immediately to a request, so you get a 'stand by'. This is not too critical with most airplanes, but in the SR it can cause big problems. Here in the States we are pretty well locked into a decel/descent point, because of the necessity of integrating our very rigid descent profile into the air traffic control system. Our current Chief of Stan/Eval, tells the story of returning from a training sortie, and running into a recalcitrant controller. As he approached his descent point, he called ATC for clearance to begin his descent. He got a 'stand by'. He called again. Same reply. Finally, after the third 'stand by', he told the controller: Sir, you don't understand Mach three flight. I CAN'T STAND BY!*

Lockheed's recon stars in a rare formation flight. The TR-1 is the latest version of the U-2. (Lockheed)

An SR-71 of Detachment 51 Flight Test from Edwards AFB formating with another black airplane.....an F-4J of Vx-4 from Point Mugu, July, 1972. (U.S. Navy)

17955 in flight. Inlet spikes will move aft up to three feet above Mach 3. Markings on underside of aircraft indicate location of reconnaissance bays (forward). (Lockheed)

SR-71 pilots regularly fly the T-38 in order to maintain proficiency. The wing's White Talons carry the SAC badge and a Yellow band adorned with four Black maltese crosses (which signify wing participation in WWI) on the tail. (Author)

(Below) Large drag chute provides effective braking action on landing. It has been deployed here before the nose wheel is on the runway. Note the deflection of the outboard elevons. Drag chute must be released before the aircraft slows to 60 knots to avoid entanglement with rudders. (USAF)

17956, the surviving two pilot SR-71B. The only other SR-71B built crashed on an approach to Beale in January 1968. An unspecified number of two pilot A-12's were built. (Lockheed)

Two Pilot
Blackbird

SR-71B Two Seater

SR-71A

The only currently operational two-pilot Blackbird is SR-71B #17956, seen here about to take on a load of JP-7 from a KC-135Q of 100th ARW. (Author)

(Above right) Close up of the twin cockpit of the SR-71B. The astro-inertial navigation star tracker is immediately behind the second cockpit. (Author)

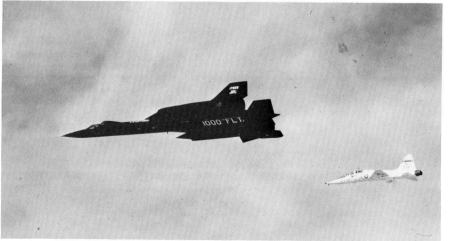

The SR-71B celebrated it's 1,000th sortie with special markings and an escort down the flightline upon it's return from the mission of January 15, 1982. Pilots on this historic flight were Lt. Col. David M. Peters and Major Gerald T. Glasser of the 1st SRS.

17962 during a fly-by at Beale in July, 1976. Aft by-pass doors are open below about Mach 1.2. (Charles B. Mayer)

(Below) Colonel Thomas S. Pugh is one of the high time SR-71 pilots, with over 900 hours. On October 15, 1973, while a member of Detachment 51 Flight Test at Palmdale, he earned a "Well Done" award for saving an SR-71 from certain destruction. The text of the "Well Done" reads as follows: "On take off, shortly after rotation and beyond the take off abort point, the left engine surged, followed by progressive failure of the second stage turbine wheel. Aircraft single-engine control at this point was marginal but the take-off was continued. After the aircraft was airborne and during gear retraction, a fire warning light illuminated, and was followed by total failure of the left hand engine turbine section. After safe single-engine speed was attained, the Commander completed engine shutdown. An intense fire in the left nacelle resulting from shrapnel damage to hydraulic, fuel and oil lines was extinguished during the shutdown procedure. Extensive damage occurred to the entire nacelle, fuselage and right rudder. Tower personnel confirmed that the fire was out. An elongated visual traffic pattern was flown in order to configure the aircraft for a single-engine landing. Landing weight was reduced and alternate systems were activated to properly configure the aircraft. A smooth landing was accomplished without further damage to the aircraft."

Exhaust of the J-58 engine, showing the aft by-pass doors from the inside and the free-floating nozzles. (John Andrews)

(Left) The secret of the SR-71's ability to maintain high cruise speeds for long periods of time is in the automatically programmed inlets, which provide up to 60% of the thrust above Mach 3. (Charles B. Mayer)

(Middle left) Slight pinching of the nacelle behind the aft inlet by-pass doors is evident in this photo. (Charles B. Mayer)

(Below Left) Crews often chalk on tails what they consider to be relevant names or messages. 17964 carried the inscription "American Beauty" in early 1979. It had just about been obliterated when this photo was taken in July, 1979. (Charles B. Mayer)

Spike tips are so sharp that they require covers to protect ground personnel. (Ted Carlson)

41

The postflight inspections performed on the SR-71 are the most extensive of any aircraft in service. There are seven postflight checklists, containing 650 separate items. It takes five structural specialists an average of 6 hours to perform these checks, which include examination of every titanium and plastic spot weld on the top of the wings. Propulsion experts spend similar time in examination of the inlets and exhausts, which are considered a part of the propulsion system, rather than the airframe. In addition to this, each aircraft is given more extensive inspections after each 25 hours of flight. Major inspections are performed every 100 and 200 hours of flight. Engines are removed and inspected at the 200 hour mark. (Charles B. Mayer, Lockheed, and Author)

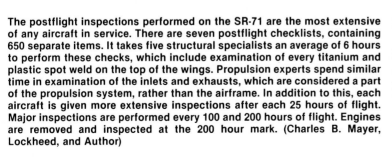

(Above) Actual paint used on the Blackbird has been quoted as being FS 35402 Indigo Blue, but it is as black as any FS black. (Lockheed)

(Below) 17964 is landing at Mildenhall in September, 1981. (H. Scharringa and P.Bennett via Norman E. Taylor)

(Above) The two most well-known forward operating locations of the SR-71s are Kadena, Okinawa, and Mildenhall, Great Britain. 17962 is preparing to depart Kadena in September, 1979.

SR-71 Crew about to board at Beale. Prior to installation of a permanent starting system in the SR-71 hangars at Beale, starter carts using twin Buick V-8's with a common drive shaft were needed to provide the starting power for the J-58. (USAF)

When the Blackbird is put on display covers are placed over all inlets, exhausts, and cockpit windows. This is Beale AFB, March, 1973. (David Menard)

Each hangar is capable of holding one Blackbird, with it's specialized support equipment. (M.C. Klaver)

Humid air makes the unusual vortices generated by the SR-71,s double delta wing visible during landing. The large wing generates a great deal of ground effect, making smooth landings routine. (Charles B. Mayer)

Blackbird crew de-planing at Offutt AFB, July, 1979. Note that ground crew have placed fans in front of the main gear in order to cool wheels and brakes. (Charles B. Mayer)

9th Wing Patch Adorned the tail of 979 in February, 1981. (Charles B. Mayer)

Shock diamonds are visible in the afterburner plume during a night engine trim check at Beale. In Mach 3 cruise flight, the tailpipe will glow white hot, while the entire aft end of the engine glows orange-red. (USAF)

The unusually stringent maintenance demands of the SR-71 require an on-the-job training cycle of 18 to 24 months before personnel are considered proficient enough to be trusted to work on the Blackbird without direct supervision. Low retention rates in the Air Force have led to a lower overall experience rate among SR maintenance personnel, which in turn has made the civilian technical representative much more important to the blackbird force. (Charles B. Mayer)

(Below)The trans-Atlantic record setter at another point in it's career carried interesting, if illegible, markings. (via David Menard)

(Below) 17973 taxies out for a mission from Utapao RTAB, Thailand, during the Vietnam War. Blackbirds flew hundreds of combat reconnaissance missions during the war, providing much of the Strategic Recce. At least one of the Blackbird losses occured on takeoff from this base when the SR-71 flew into a thunderstorm. (USAF)

The *Rapid Rabbit* refuelling from a KC-135Q. Though the JP-7 is kept in separate tanks in the tanker, crew members report that they are able to burn it if necessary in the tanker engines. (USAF)

17974 has the distinction of flying more combat missions during the Vietnam War than any other SR-71, hence the sobriquet *Ichi Ban.* It was still flying as of January, 1982, and it's crew chief reports that it is one of the best of the Blackbirds. (USAF via Norm Taylor)

979 taxies in, post-mission. Note the drag cute compartment doors remain open after chute is released. Ground personnel are warned to keep clear of the SR until at least 30 minutes after it has landed, it takes that long to cool the airframe. (Charles B. Mayer)

The one and only SR-71C was built from bits and pieces of an engineering mock-up and salvaged parts after half the SR-71B force was lost in the January 1968 crash of 951. Known as *The Bastard,* it was not extensively used, and has been in storage for several years. (Brian Rogers via Jerry Geer)

Col. Robert L. "Silver Fox" Stephens, the first military pilot to fly the Blackbird, led the YF-12 record setters in the 1965 record runs, is seen here with one of his Fire Control Officers, LtCol. Daniel Andre. (Lockheed)

The entire 1965 record setting YF-12A group, from left to right: Cooney, Daniel, Stephens, Andre, Warner. (Lockheed)

SR-71 World Records

OFFICIAL ABSOLUTE WORLD RECORDS, 31 DECEMBER 1976
(Maximum Performance in any Class)

28 July 76	ALTITUDE IN HORIZONTAL FLIGHT Capt Robert C. Helt, USAF	25,929.031 Meters 85,068.997 Feet
28 July 76	SPEED OVER A CLOSED COURSE Capt Eldon W. Joersz, USAF	3,529.56 KPH 2,193.167 MPH
27 July 76	SPEED OVER A CLOSED CIRCUIT Maj Adolphus H. Bledsoe, Jr., USAF	3,367.221KPH 2,092,294 MPH

Class C-1, Group III (Jet) Without Payload

28 July 76	ALTITUDE IN HORIZONTAL FLIGHT Capt Rober C. Helt, USAF	25,929.031 Meters 85,068.997 Feet
28 July 76	SPEED OVER A 15/25 KM CLOSED COURSE Capt Eldon W. Joersz, USAF	3,529.56 KPH 2,193.167 MPH
27 July 76	CLOSED CIRCUIT - 1,000 KMS SPEED Maj ADolphus H. Bledsoe, Jr., USAF	3,367.221 KPH 2,092.294 MPH

Class C-1, Group III (Jet) with Payload (1,000 Kilograms)

| 27 July 76 | CLOSED CIRUIT - 1,000 KMS SPEED Maj Adolphus H. Bledsoe Jr., USAF | |

Class C-1, Group III (Jet)

| 1 Sept 74 | SPEED OVER A RECOGNIZED COURSE - NEW YORK TO LONDON Maj James V. Sullivan, USAF | 2,908.026 KPH 1,806.964 MPH |
| 13 Sept 74 | SPEED OVER A RECOGNIZED COURSE - LONDON TO LOS ANGELES Capt Harold B. Adams, USAF | 2,310.353 KPH 1,435.587 MPH |

972 touching down at Farnborough after it's New York to London record flight. (M.C. Klaver)

(Below) The Blackbird taxies out for a record attempt. (Charles B. Mayer)

(Below left) Captain Robert C. Helt climbs aboard the SR-71 he flew to the absolute world altitude record.(USAF via Charles. B. Mayer)

The SR-71's used for the record runs of 1976 carried markings that made it easier for FAI representatives to track them from their ground positions at Edwards AFB. (Charles B. Mayer)

squadron/signal's
Vietnam Studies Group

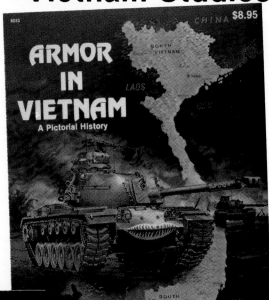

$6.95

PHANTOM II
A Pictorial History of the McDonnell Douglas F-4 Phantom II
by Lou Drendel

squadron/signal publications

CHINA $8.95

NORTH VIETNAM

ARMOR IN VIETNAM
A Pictorial History

LAOS

SOUTH VIETNAM

squadron/signal publi

$8.95

AIR WAR over Southeast Asia
A Pictorial Record
Vol. 2 1967-1970
By Lou Drendel

Coming Soo

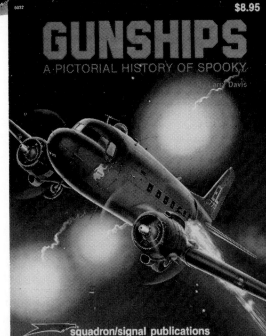

$8.95

GUNSHIPS
A PICTORIAL HISTORY OF SPOOKY
by Davis

squadron/signal publications

$8.95

AIR WAR over Southeast Asia
A Pictorial Record
Vol. 1 1962-1966
By Lou Drendel

U.S. AIR FORCE

squadron/signal publications

$8

AIR WAR over Southeast Asia
A Pictorial Record
Vol. 3 1971-1975
By Lou Drendel

squadron/signal publications